The Funny French Sentences

Workbook for Kids

KINGSNORTH KIDS

The Funny French Sentences Workbook for Kids

ISBN 978-1-916922-07-5 **(paperback)**

Kingsnorth Kids is an imprint of Kingsnorth Publishing.

Contents

Note to Parents and Carers

This book has been designed to help children learn how to conjugate French verbs in a fun, simple and, above all, hands-on way. Ideal for kinaesthetic learners, children can physically create the sentence they want in English, before flipping it over and seeing how it is translated into French. This means that they will get used to how the verb changes depending on the subject (pronoun) without even noticing!

All words come complete with pronunciations, which means that, not only can they read and write the French sentence, they can also learn to say it, thereby getting used to how French words sound.

Each unit contains short, easily learnable word lists, full of fun and engaging vocabulary, specially selected to fit together in various ways. Children can let their imaginations run wild exploring different ways of combining them to make a whole range of funny sentences!

We suggest that a parent or carer cuts out the cards for each unit to avoid words being cut off by little hands (You may wish to use envelopes to keep the cards safe in case your child wishes to revisit a verb and refresh their learning). After that, you can safely leave older children to get on with creating their own funny French sentences!

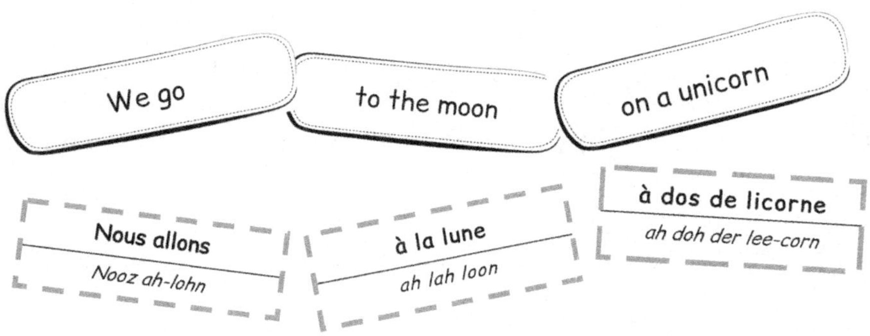

Each unit comes with three challenge sentences for them to create, to introduce them to the sentence construction in that particular unit, followed by space for them to record their own creations.

Additionally, children are taught how to conjugate other regular verbs, giving them the confidence to continue conjugating verbs independently!

We really hope your child enjoys this book!

French Pronouns

When compared to English, French pronouns can seem a little complicated. For example, in English, we only have six main pronouns to learn when first conjugating verbs:

I, you, he, she, we and **they**

In French, there are several more and some of these change, depending on the **amount of people**, and their **gender**.

For example, there are different versions of **'You'**, depending on if you are talking about **one person**, or **more than one person** (singular or plural). Confusingly, the plural version of 'You' is also used to show respect to someone you don't know very well:

Tu	You (singular - informal)
Vous	You (plural - informal)
Vous	You (singular or plural - formal)

Unlike in English, **'They'**, too, changes depending on the gender of the people being discussed. One thing to note is that if ANY of the people being discussed are male, then the male form is used. The female form is ONLY used when all the people are female.

Ils	They (all male OR male and female)
Elles	They (all female)

Now, let's have a look at these pronouns and learn when they are used, so that you can identify them when making your sentences!

Pronoun	Meaning	Pronunciation	When to Use
Je	*I*	*jher*	When talking about **yourself.**
Tu	*You*	*too*	When talking to **one** person **you know well.**
Il	*He*	*eel*	When talking about **one male**
Elle	*She*	*el*	When talking about **one female.**
Nous	*We*	*noo*	When talking about **yourself** and any others.
Vous	*You*	*voo*	When talking to **more than one** person OR formally, even to only one person.
Ils	*They*	*eel*	When talking about **two or more** people, where **at least one** of them is **male.**
Elles	*They*	*el*	When talking about **two or more females (ALL female).**

Now...

Are you ready to start writing funny sentences in Français?

Let's begin!

Être (et-ruh) To Be

Type of verb:
Irregular

Anglais	Français	Say it!
I am	Je suis	*Jher swee*
You are (informal singular)	Tu es	*Too eh*
He is	Il est	*Eel eh*
She is	Elle est	*El eh*
We are	Nous sommes	*Noo som*
You are (formal singular and ALL plurals)	Vous êtes	*Vooz et*
They are (plural, if any are males)	Ils sont	*Eel sohn*
They are (plural, if all are female)	Elles sont	*El sohn*

Extra Vocabulary		
on the farm	à la ferme	*ah lah fairm*
on Mars	sur Mars	*s'your Marhss*
at the party	à la fête	*ah lah fet*
at the swimming pool	à la piscine	*ah lah pee-seen*
to dance with	pour danser avec	*poorh don-seh ah-vek*
to play hide-and-seek with	pour jouer au cache-cache avec	*poorh jhoo-eh oh cash-cash ah-vek*
to ski with	pour skier avec	*poorh skee-eh ah-vek*
some aliens	des extraterrestres	*dehz extrah-ter-hess-truh*
the dolphins	les dauphins	*leh doh-fahn*
some monkeys	des singes	*deh sanjh*

I am	on the farm
You are (Informal singular)	on Mars
He is	at the party
She is	at the pool
We are	to dance with
You are (Formal singular and ALL plurals)	to play hide-and-seek with
They are (Plural, where at least one is male)	to ski with
They are (Plural, where all are female)	some aliens
the dolphins	some monkeys

à la ferme	**Je suis**
ah lah fairm	*Jher swee*
sur Mars	**Tu es**
s'your Marhss	*Too eh*
à la fet	**Il est**
ah lah fet	*Eel eh*
à la piscine	**Elle est**
ah lah pee-seen	*El eh*
pour danser avec	**Nous sommes**
poorh don-seh ah-vek	*Noo som*
pour jouer au cache-cache avec	**Vous êtes**
poorh jhoo-eh oh cash-cash ah-vek	*Vooz et*
pour skier avec	**Ils sont**
poorh skee-eh ah-vek	*Eel sohn*
des extraterrestres	**Elles sont**
dehz extrah-ter-hess-truh	*El sohn*
des singes	**les dauphins**
deh sanjh	*leh doh-fahn*

Funny Sentences Using 'Être'

Can you write these funny sentences in French?

I am on Mars to ski with some monkeys.

She is at the party to dance with some aliens.

He is at the pool to play hide-and-seek with the dolphins.

Now, can you write your own? Don't forget to make them funny!

Avoir *(av-warh)* To Have

Type of verb:
Irregular

Anglais	Français	Say it!
I have	J'ai	*Jheh*
You have (informal singular)	Tu as	*Too ah*
He has	Il a	*Eel ah*
She has	Elle a	*El ah*
We have	Nous avons	*Nooz ah-vohn*
You have (formal singular and ALL plurals)	Vous avez	*Vooz ah-veh*
They have (plural, if any are males)	Ils ont	*Eelz ohn*
They have (plural, if all are female)	Elles ont	*Elz ohn*

Extra Vocabulary		
some elephants	des éléphants	*dehz eh-leh-fohn*
some hippos	des hippopotames	*dehz ee-poh-pot-am*
some socks	des chaussettes	*deh shoh-set*
some soldiers	des soldats	*deh sol-dah*
who dance ballet	qui dansent le ballet	*kee dohns ler bah-leh*
who hide	qui se cachent	*kee ser cash*
who knit	qui tricotent	*kee tree-kot*
in the wardrobe	dans l'armoire	*dohn larm-wah*
on the roof	sur le toit	*s'your ler twah*
under the bed	sous le lit	*soo ler lee*

I have	some elephants
You have (Informal singular)	some hippos
He has	some socks
She has	some soldiers
We have	who dance ballet
You have (Formal singular and ALL plurals)	who hide
They have (Plural, where at least one is male)	who knit
They have (Plural, where all are female)	in the wardrobe
under the bed	on the roof

des éléphants	**J'ai**
dehz eh-leh-fohn	*Jheh*
des hippopotames	**Tu as**
dehz ee-poh-pot-am	*Too ah*
des chaussettes	**Il a**
deh shoh-set	*Eel ah*
des soldats	**Elle a**
deh sol-dah	*El ah*
qui dansent le ballet	**Nous avons**
kee dohns ler bah-leh	*Nooz ah-vohn*
qui se cachent	**Vous avez**
kee ser cash	*Vooz ah-veh*
qui tricotent	**Ils ont**
kee tree-cot	*Eelz ohn*
dans l'armoire	**Elles ont**
dohn larhm-wah	*Elz ohn*
sur le toit	**sous le lit**
s'your ler twah	*soo ler lee*

Funny Sentences Using 'Avoir'

I have some elephants under the bed.

They (all girls) have some socks who dance ballet on the roof.

You (plural) have some hippos who hide in the wardrobe.

Now, can you write your own? Don't forget to make them funny!

Faire *(fairh)*

To Make/Do (also, in some instances, to play, take, go, be, etc.)

Type of verb:
Irregular

Anglais	Français	Say it!
I make/do	**Je fais**	*Jher feh*
You make/do (informal singular)	**Tu fais**	*Too feh*
He makes/does	**Il fait**	*Eel feh*
She makes/does	**Elle fait**	*El feh*
We make/do	**Nous faisons**	*Noo feh-zohn*
You make/do (formal singular and ALL plurals)	**Vous faites**	*Voo fet*
They make/do (plural, if any are males)	**Ils font**	*Eel fohn*
They make/do (plural, if all are female)	**Elles font**	*El fohn*

Extra Vocabulary		
the cooking	la cuisine	*lah quee-zeen*
the shopping	les courses	*leh corse*
the washing up	la vaisselle	*lah veh-sel*
noise	du bruit	*dew brwee*
a trip	un voyage	*uhn v'wah-yahj*
with	avec	*ah-vek*
an astronaut	un astronaute	*uhn ah-stroh-naut*
a crocodile	un crocodile	*uhn croc-oh-deel*
a film star	une vedette de cinéma	*oon veh-det der see-neh-mah*
a robot	un robot	*uhn roh-boh*

I make/I do	the cooking
You make/You do (Informal singular)	the shopping
He makes/He does	the washing up
She makes/She does	some noise
We make/We do	a trip
You make/You do (Formal singular and ALL plurals)	with
They make/They do (Plural, where at least one is male)	an astronaut
They make/They do (Plural, where all are female)	a crocodile
a robot	a film star

la cuisine	**Je fais**
lah quee-zeen	*Jher feh*
les courses	**Tu fais**
leh corse	*Too feh*
la vaisselle	**Il fait**
lah veh-sel	*Eel feh*
du bruit	**Elle fait**
dew brwee	*El feh*
un voyage	**Nous faisons**
uhn v'wah-yahj	*Noo feh-zohn*
avec	**Vous faites**
ah-vek	*Voo fet*
un astronaute	**Ils font**
uhn ah-stroh-naut	*Eel fohn*
un crocodile	**Elles font**
uhn croc-oh-deel	*El fohn*
une vedette de cinéma	**un robot**
oon veh-det der see-neh-mah	*uhn roh-boh*

Funny Sentences Using 'Faire'

I make some noise with a robot.

They (all boys) do the shopping with an astronaut.

You (singular) make a trip with a crocodile.

Now, can you write your own? Don't forget to make them funny!

Aller (ah-leh) To Go

Type of verb:
Irregular

Anglais	Français	Say it!
I go	Je vais	*Jher veh*
You go (informal singular)	Tu vas	*Too vah*
He goes	Il va	*Eel vah*
She goes	Elle va	*El vah*
We go	Nous allons	*Nooz ah-lohn*
You go (formal singular and ALL plurals)	Vous allez	*Vooz ah-leh*
They go (plural, if any are males)	Ils vont	*Eel vohn*
They go (plural, if all are female)	Elles vont	*El vohn*

Extra Vocabulary		
to the shops	aux magasins	*oh mah-gah-zahn*
to the moon	à la Lune	*a lah loon*
to school	à l'école	*ah leh-coll*
to the library	à la bibliothèque	*ah lah bee-blee-o-teck*
to the beach	à la plage	*ah lah plajh*
to the mountain	à la montagne	*ah lah mon-tan-yer*
on an adventure	à l'aventure	*ah lah-vohn-t'ure*
on a scooter	en trottinette	*ohn trot-ee-net*
on a unicorn	à dos de licorne	*ah doh der lee-corn*
on vacation/holiday	en vacances	*ohn va-conss*

I go	to the beach
You go (Informal singular)	to the library
He goes	to the moon
She goes	to the mountain
We go	to school
You go (Formal singular and ALL plurals)	to the shops
They go (Plural, where at least one is male)	on an adventure
They go (Plural, where all are female)	on a scooter
on a unicorn	on vacation/holiday

à la plage	**Je vais**
ah lah plajh	*Jher veh*
à la bibliothèque	**Tu vas**
ah lah bee-blee-oh-teck	*Too vah*
à la Lune	**Il va**
ah lah loon	*Eel vah*
à la montagne	**Elle va**
ah lah mon-tan-yer	*El vah*
à l'école	**Nous allons**
ah leh-coll	*Nooz ah-lohn*
aux magasins	**Vous allez**
oh mah-gah-zahn	*Vooz ah-leh*
à l'aventure	**Ils vont**
ah lah-vohn-t'ure	*Eel vohn*
en trottinette	**Elles vont**
ohn trot-ee-net	*El vohn*
en vacances	**à dos de licorne**
ohn va-conss	*ah doh der lee-corn*

Funny Sentences Using 'Aller'

Can you write these funny sentences in French?

I go to the moon.

____

You (singular) go on holiday to the library.

____

He goes to school on a unicorn.

____

Now, can you write your own? Don't forget to make them silly!

____

____

____

____

____

Dire (deerh) To Say

Type of verb: Irregular

Anglais	Français	Say it!
I say	Je dis	*Jher dee*
You say (informal singular)	Tu dis	*Too dee*
He says	Il dit	*Eel dee*
She saya	Elle dit	*El dee*
We say	Nous disons	*Noo dee-zohn*
You say (formal singular and ALL plurals)	Vous dites	*Voo deet*
They say (plural, if any are males)	Ils disent	*Eel deez*
They say (plural, if all are female)	Elles disent	*El deez*

Extra Vocabulary		
hi	salut	*sah-loo*
hello	bonjour	*bohn-jhorh*
goodbye	au revoir	*oh rer-v'warh*
jokes (as in 'tells jokes')	des blagues	*deh blahg*
to the clown	au clown	*oh cloon*
to the narwhal	au narval	*oh nahr-val*
to the vampire	au vampire	*oh vom-peerh*
with the red nose	au nez rouge	*oh neh roojh*
with the pink eyes	aux yeux roses	*ohz yer roz*
with the green hair	aux cheveux verts	*oh sher-ver vairh*

I say	hi
You say (Informal singular)	hello
He says	goodbye
She says	jokes
We say	to the clown
You say (Formal singular and ALL plurals)	to the narwhal
They say (Plural, where at least one is male)	to the vampire
They say (Plural, where all are female)	with the red nose
with the green hair	with the pink eyes

salut	**Je dis**
sah-loo	*Jher dee*
bonjour	**Tu dis**
bohn-jhorh	*Too dee*
au revoir	**Il dit**
oh rer-v'warh	*Eel dee*
des blagues	**Elle dit**
deh blahg	*El dee*
au clown	**Nous disons**
oh cloon	*Noo dee-zohn*
au narval	**Vous dites**
oh nahr-val	*Voo deet*
au vampire	**Ils disent**
oh vom-peerh	*Eel deez*
au nez rouge	**Elles disent**
oh neh roojh	*El deez*
aux yeux roses	**aux cheveux verts**
ohz yer roz	*oh sher-ver vairh*

Funny Sentences Using 'Dire'

He tells (says) jokes to the vampire.

She says hello to the narwhal with green hair.

You (formal) say hi to the clown with pink eyes.

Now, can you write your own?
Don't forget to make them funny!

Vouloir *(vool-warh)* To Want

Type of verb:
Irregular

Anglais	Français	Say it!
I want	**Je veux**	*Jher ver*
You want (informal singular)	**Tu veux**	*Too ver*
He wants	**Il veut**	*Eel ver*
She wants	**Elle veut**	*El ver*
We want	**Nous voulons**	*Noo voo-lohn*
You want (formal singular and ALL plurals)	**Vous voulez**	*Voo voo-leh*
They want (plural, if any are males)	**Ils veulent**	*Eel verl-uh (quick 'uh')*
They want (plural, if all are female)	**Elles veulent**	*El verl-uh (quick 'uh')*

Extra Vocabulary		
to sing	chanter	*shon-teh*
to dance	danser	*dohn-seh*
to skate	patiner	*pah-tee-neh*
to skip (along)	sautiller	*soh-tee-eh*
with	avec	*ah-vek*
some gorillas	des gorilles	*deh gohr-eel*
some mermaids	des sirènes	*deh see-hren*
some pirates	des pirates	*deh pee-hrat*
some giraffes	des girafes	*jhee-hraf*
some parrots	des perroquets	*deh peh-roh-keh*

I want	to sing
You want (Informal singular)	to dance
He wants	to skate
She wants	to skip
We want	with
You want (Formal singular and ALL plurals)	some gorillas
They want (Plural, where at least one is male)	some mermaids
They want (Plural, where all are female)	some pirates
some parrots	some giraffes

chanter	**Je veux**
shon-teh	*Jher ver*
danser	**Tu veux**
dohn-seh	*Too ver*
patiner	**Il veut**
pah-tee-neh	*Eel ver*
sautiller	**Elle veut**
soh-tee-eh	*El ver*
avec	**Nous voulons**
ah-vek	*Noo voo-lohn*
des gorilles	**Vous voulez**
deh goh-reel	*Voo voo-leh*
des sirènes	**Ils veulent**
deh see-hren	*Eel verl-uh (quick uh)*
des pirates	**Elles veulent**
deh pee-hrat	*El verl-uh (quick uh)*
des girafes	**des perroquets**
deh jhee-hraf	*deh peh-roh-keh*

Funny Sentences Using 'Vouloir'

I want to skip with some pirates.

They (group with one boy) want to skate with some mermaids.

We want to sing with some gorillas.

Now, can you write your own? Don't forget to make them funny!

Pouvoir *(poov-warh)* To be able to

Type of verb:
Irregular

Anglais	Français	Say it!
I can	Je peux	*Jher per*
You can (informal singular)	Tu peux	*Too per*
He can	Il peut	*Eel per*
She can	Elle peut	*El per*
We can	Nous pouvons	*Noo poov-ohn*
You can (formal singular and ALL plurals)	Vous pouvez	*Voo poov-eh*
They can (plural, if any are males)	Ils peuvent	*Eel purv*
They can (plural, if all are female)	Elles peuvent	*El purv*

Extra Vocabulary		
fly	voler	*vol-eh*
jump	sauter	*soh-teh*
run	courir	*coo-hreehr*
swim	nager	*nah-jheh*
like a butterfly	comme un papillon	*com uhn pah-pee-ohn*
like a camel	comme un chameau	*com uhn shah-moh*
a snake	comme un serpent	*com uhn sairh-pon*
a whale	comme une baleine	*com oon bah-len*
in the sky	dans le ciel	*dohn ler see-el*
in the sea	dans la mer	*dohn lah mairh*

I can	fly
You can (Informal singular)	jump
He can	run
She can	swim
We can	like a butterfly
You can (Formal singular and ALL plurals)	like a camel
They can (Plural, where at least one is male)	like a snake
They can (Plural, where all are female)	like a whale
in the sky	in the sea

voler	**Je peux**
voh-leh	*Jher per*
sauter	**Tu peux**
soh-teh	*Too per*
courir	**Il peut**
coo-hreehr	*Eel per*
nager	**Elle peut**
nah-jheh	*El per*
comme un papillon	**Nous pouvons**
com uhn pah-pee-on	*Noo poov-ohn*
comme un chameau	**Vous pouvez**
com uhn shah-moh	*Voo poov-eh*
comme un serpent	**Ils peuvent**
com uhn sairh-pon	*Eel purv*
comme une baleine	**Elles peuvent**
com oon bah-len	*El purv*
dans la mer	**dans le ciel**
dohn lah mairh	*dohn ler see-el*

Funny Sentences Using 'Pouvoir'

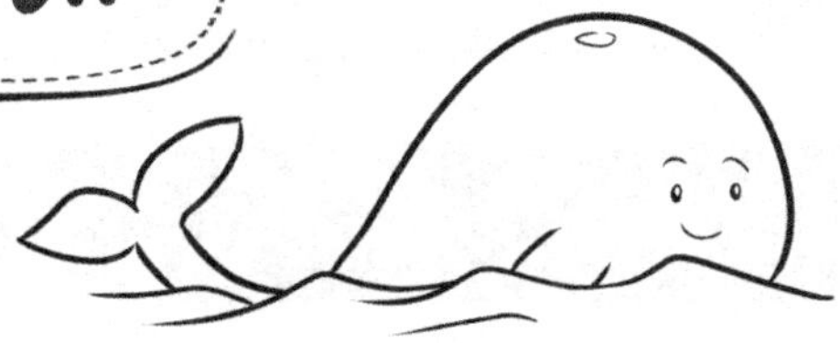

He can fly like a snake.

You (informal) can swim like a butterfly in the sea.

She can run like a whale in the sky.

Now, can you write your own?
Don't forget to make them funny!

Manger *(mohn-jheh)* To eat

Type of verb:
Irregular

Anglais	Français	Say it!
I eat	**Je mange**	*Jher monjh*
You eat (informal singular)	**Tu manges**	*Too monjh*
He eats	**Il mange**	*Eel monjh*
She eats	**Elle mange**	*El monjh*
We eat	**Nous mongeons**	*Noo monjh-ohn*
You eat (formal singular and ALL plurals)	**Vous mangez**	*Voo monjh-eh*
They eat (plural, if any are males)	**Ils mangent**	*Eel monjh*
They eat (plural, if all are female)	**Elles mangent**	*El monjh*

Extra Vocabulary		
(some) mud	de la boue	*der lah boo*
(some) fish	du poisson	*dew pwah-sohn*
(some) potatoes	des pommes de terre	*deh pom der tairh*
(some) eggs	des œufs	*dehz erf*
(some) cheese	du fromage	*dew from-arjh*
(some) ice cream	de la glace	*der lah glas*
(some) cake	du gateau	*dew gah-toh*
(some) bananas	des bananes	*deh bah-nahn*
with	avec	*ah-vek*
and	et	*eh*

I eat	mud
You eat (Informal singular)	fish
He eats	potatoes
She eats	eggs
We eat	cheese
You eat (Formal singular and ALL plurals)	ice cream
They eat (Plural, where at least one is male)	cake
They eat (Plural, where all are female)	bananas
with	and

de la boue	**Je mange**
der lah boo	*Jher monjh*
du poisson	**Tu manges**
dew pwah-sohn	*Too monjh*
des pommes de terre	**Il mange**
deh pom der tairh	*Eel monjh*
des œufs	**Elle mange**
dehz erf	*El monjh*
du fromage	**Nous mangeons**
dew froh-marjh	*Noo monjh-ohn*
de la glace	**Vous mangez**
der lah glas	*Voo monjh-eh*
du gateau	**Ils mangent**
dew gah-toh	*Eel monjh*
des bananes	**Elles mangent**
deh bah-nahn	*El monjh*
et	**avec**
eh	*ah-vek*

Funny Sentences Using 'Manger'

I eat cheese and ice cream.

She eats bananas with fish.

You (formal) eat cake and potatoes with mud.

Now, can you write your own? Don't forget to make them funny!

Boire (Bwarh) To drink

Type of verb: Irregular

Anglais	Français	Say it!
I drink	**Je bois**	*Jher bwah*
You drink (informal singular)	**Tu bois**	*Too bwah*
He drinks	**Il boit**	*Eel bwah*
She drinks	**Elle boit**	*El bwah*
We drink	**Nous buvons**	*Noo boo-vohn*
You drink (formal singular and ALL plurals)	**Vous buvez**	*Voo boo-veh*
They drink (plural, if any are males)	**Ils boivent**	*Eel bwahv*
They drink (plural, if all are female)	**Elles boivent**	*El bwahv*

Extra Vocabulary		
(some) coffee	**du café**	*dew cah-feh*
(some) tea	**du thé**	*dew teh*
(some) orange juice	**du jus d'orange**	*dew joo d'oh-ronjh*
(some) hot chocolate	**du chocolat chaud**	*dew shoh-coh-la choh*
(some) milk	**du lait**	*dew leh*
from (literally, though, 'in')	**dans**	*dohn*
a bucket	**un seau**	*uhn soh*
a watering can	**un arrosoir**	*uhn ah-roz-warh*
a fish bowl	**un bocal à poissons**	*uhn boh-cal ah pwah-sohn*
a frying pan	**une poêle**	*oon poh-el*

I drink	coffee
You drink (Informal singular)	tea
He drinks	orange juice
She drinks	hot chocolate
We drink	milk
You drink (Formal singular and ALL plurals)	from
They drink (Plural, where at least one is male)	a bucket
They drink (Plural, where all are female)	a watering can
a frying pan	a fish bowl

du café	Je bois
dew cah-feh	*Jher bwah*
du thé	Tu bois
dew teh	*Too bwah*
du jus d'orange	Il boit
dew joo d'oh-ronjh	*Eel bwah*
du chocolat chaud	Elle boit
dew shoh-coh-la shoh	*El bwah*
du lait	Nous buvons
dew leh	*Noo boo-vohn*
dans	Vous buvez
dohn	*Voo boo-veh*
un seau	Ils boivent
uhn soh	*Eel bwahv*
un arrosoir	Elles boivent
uhn ah-roz-wahr	*El bwahv*
un bocal à poissons	une poêle
uhn boh-cal ah pwah-sohn	*oon poh-el*

Funny Sentences Using 'Boire'

I drink milk from a watering can.

You (informal singular) drink coffee from a fish bowl.

They (all girls) drink tea from a frying pan.

Now, can you write your own?
Don't forget to make them funny!

Voir (vwarh) To see

Type of verb:
Irregular

Anglais	Français	Say it!
I see	Je vois	*Jher vwah*
You see (informal singular)	Tu vois	*Too vwah*
He sees	Il voit	*Eel vwah*
She sees	Elle voit	*El vwah*
We see	Nous voyons	*Noo vwah-yohn*
You see (formal singular and ALL plurals)	Vous voyez	*Voo vwah-yeh*
They see (plural, if any are males)	Ils voient	*Eel vwah*
They see (plural, if all are female)	Elles voient	*El vwah*

Extra Vocabulary		
a lion	un lion	*uhn lee-ohn*
a zebra	une zèbre	*oon zeb-ruh (quick 'uh')*
a sloth	un paresseux	*uhn pah-ress-er*
a jellyfish	une méduse	*oon meh-d'yoos*
doing yoga	faire du yoga	*fairh dew yoh-gah*
tap dancing	faire des claquettes	*fairh deh clah-ket*
playing piano	jouer du piano	*jhoo-eh dew pee-ah-no*
in the moonlight	au clair de lune	*oh clairh der loon*
in the rain	sous la pluie	*soo lah pl'wee*
in the bath	dans le bain	*dohn ler bahn*

I see	a lion
You see (Informal singular)	a zebra
He sees	a sloth
She sees	a jellyfish
We see	doing yoga
You see (Formal singular and ALL plurals)	tap dancing
They see (Plural, where at least one is male)	playing piano
They see (Plural, where all are female)	in the moonlight
in the bath	in the rain

un lion	**Je vois**
uhn lee-ohn	*Jher vwah*
une zèbre	**Tu vois**
oon zeb-ruh (quick ruh)	*Too vwah*
un paresseux	**Il voit**
uhn pah-res-er	*Eel vwah*
une méduse	**Elle voit**
oon meh-d'yoos	*El vwah*
faire du yoga	**Nous voyons**
fairh dew yoh-gah	*Noo vwah-yohn*
faire des claquettes	**Vous voyez**
fairh deh clah-ket	*Voo vwah-yeh*
jouer du piano	**Ils voient**
jhoo-eh dew pee-ah-no	*Eel vwah*
au clair de lune	**Elle voient**
oh clair der loon	*El vwah*
dans la pluie	**dans le bain**
dohn lah pl'wee	*dohn ler bahn*

Funny Sentences Using 'Voir'

I see a sloth playing piano.

He sees a lion doing yoga in the moonlight.

They (all boys) see a jellyfish tapdancing in the bath.

Now, can you write your own?
Don't forget to make them funny!

Devoir *(der-vwarh)* To have to

Type of verb:
Irregular

Anglais	Français	Say it!
I must	Je dois	*Jher dwah*
You must (informal singular)	Tu dois	*Too dwah*
He must	Il doit	*Eel dwah*
She must	Elle doit	*El dwah*
We must	Nous devons	*Noo der-vohn*
You must (formal singular and ALL plurals)	Vous devez	*Voo der-veh*
They must (plural, if any are males)	Ils doivent	*Eel dwahv*
They must (plural, if all are female)	Elles doivent	*El dwahv*

Extra Vocabulary		
(to) wear	porter	*porh-teh*
a ball gown	une robe de bal	*oon rhob der bahl*
a crown	une couronne	*oon coor-hon*
flippers	des palmes	*deh pahlm*
slippers	des pantoufles	*deh pohn-too-fl*
a football kit	un kit de football	*uhn keet der foot-bool*
a suit of armor	une armure	*oon arhm-ure*
to the party	à la fête	*ah lah fet*
to the dentist	chez le dentiste	*sheh ler dohn-teest*
and	et	*eh*

I must	wear
You must (Informal singular)	a ball gown
He must	a crown
She must	flippers
We must	slippers
You must (Formal singular and ALL plurals)	a football kit
They must (Plural, where at least one is male)	a suit of armor
They must (Plural, where all are female)	to the party
and	to the dentist

porter	Je dois
porh-teh	*Jher dwah*
une robe de bal	**Tu dois**
oon rhob der bahl	*Too dwah*
une couronne	**Il doit**
oon coor-hon	*Eel dwah*
des palmes	**Elle doit**
deh pahlm	*El dwah*
des pantoufles	**Nous devons**
deh pohn-too-fl	*Noo der-vohn*
un kit de football	**Vous devez**
uhn keet der foot-bool	*Voo der-veh*
une armure	**Ils doivent**
oon arhm-ure	*Eel dwahv*
à la fête	**Elles doivent**
ah lah fet	*El dwahv*
chez le dentiste	**et**
sheh ler dohn-teest	*eh*

Funny Sentences Using 'Devoir'

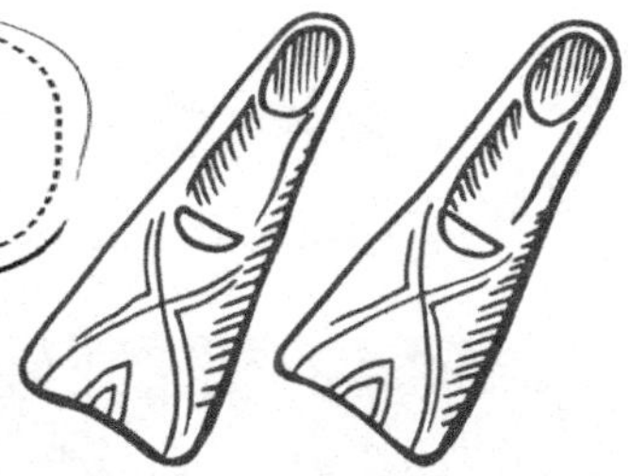

I must wear a suit of armour and flippers.

They (all boys) must wear a ball gown and slippers to the party.

We must wear a football kit, slippers and a crown to the dentist.

Now, can you write your own? Don't forget to make them funny!

Aimer (ehm-eh) To like/love

Type of verb:
Regular -er

Anglais	Français	Say it!
I like/love	J'aime	*Jhehm*
You like/love (informal singular)	Tu aimes	*Too ehm*
He likes/loves	Il aime	*Eel ehm*
She likes/loves	Elle aime	*El ehm*
We like/love	Nous aimons	*Nooz ehm-ohn*
You like/love (formal singular and ALL plurals)	Vous aimez	*Vooz ehm-eh*
They like/love (plural, if any are males)	Ils aiment	*Eel ehm*
They like/love (plural, if all are female)	Elles aiment	*El ehm*

Extra Vocabulary		
the feel	la sensation	*lah sohn-sass-ee-ohn*
the smell	l'odeur	*loh-derh*
the taste	le goût	*ler goo*
of pigs	des cochons	*deh coh-shohn*
of snails	des escargots	*dehz es-cahr-goh*
of spiders	des araignées	*dehz ah-rehn-yeh*
when	quand	*cohnd*
it rains/it is raining	il pleut	*eel pler*
it is sunny	il fait beau	*eel feh boh*
it snows/it is snowing	il neige	*eel nejh*

I love	the feel
You love (Informal singular)	the smell
He loves	the taste
She loves	of pigs
We love	of snails
You love (Formal singular and ALL plurals)	of spiders
They love (Plural, where at least one is male)	when
They love (Plural, where all are female)	it is raining
it is snowing	it is sunny

la sensation	**J'aime**
lah sohn-sass-ee-ohn	*Jhehm*
l'odeur	**Tu aimes**
loh-derh	*Too ehm*
le goût	**Il aime**
ler goo	*Eel ehm*
des cochons	**Elle aime**
deh coh-shohn	*El ehm*
des escargots	**Nous aimons**
dehz es-cahr-goh	*Nooz ehm-ohn*
des araignées	**Vous aimez**
dehs ah-rehn-yeh	*Vooz ehm-eh*
quand	**Ils aiment**
cohnd	*Eel ehm*
il pleut	**Elles aiment**
eel pler	*El ehm*
il fait beau	**il neige**
eel feh boh	*eel nejh*

Funny Sentences Using 'Aimer'

I love the smell of pigs when it's snowing.

They (all girls) love the feel of snails when it's sunny.

You (formal) love the taste of spiders when it's raining.

Now write your own sentences. How disgusting can you make them?

Demander *(deh-mon-deh)* To ask/ask for

Type of verb:
Regular -er

Anglais	Français	Say it!
I ask	Je demande	*Jher deh-mond*
You ask (informal singular)	Tu demandes	*Too deh-mond*
He asks	Il demande	*Eel deh-mond*
She asks	Elle demande	*El deh-mond*
We ask	Nous demandons	*Noo deh-mon-dohn*
You ask (formal singular and ALL plurals)	Vous demandez	*Voo deh-mon-deh*
They ask (plural, if any are males)	Ils demandent	*Eel deh-mond*
They ask (plural, if all are female)	Elles demandent	*El deh-mond*

Extra Vocabulary		
a tiger	un tigre	*uhn teeg-ruh (quick ruh)*
a trumpet	une trompette	*oon tromp-et*
a dinosaur	un dinosaure	*uhn dee-noh-sorh*
a rainbow	un arc-en-ciel	*uhn arc-ohn-see-el*
and ketchup	et du ketchup	*eh dew ketch-oop*
with fries	avec des frites	*ah-vek deh freet*
on toast	sur du pain grillé	*s'your dew pahn gree-eh*
for breakfast	pour le petit-déjeuner	*por ler p'tee deh-jher-neh*
for dinner	pour le dîner	*por ler dee-neh*
for dessert	pour le dessert	*por ler deh-sairh*

I ask for	a tiger
You ask for (Informal singular)	a trumpet
He asks for	a dinosaur
She asks for	a rainbow
We ask for	and ketchup
You ask for (Formal singular and ALL plurals)	with fries
They ask for (Plural, where at least one is male)	on toast
They ask for (Plural, where all are female)	for breakfast
for dessert	for dinner

un tigre	Je demande
uhn teeg-ruh	*Jher deh-mond*
une trompette	Tu demandes
oon tromp-et	*Too deh-mond*
un dinosaure	Il demande
uhn dee-noh-sorh	*Eel deh-mond*
un arc-en-ciel	Elle demande
uhn arc-ohn-see-el	*El deh-mond*
et du ketchup	Nous demandons
eh dew ketch-oop	*Noo deh-mon-dohn*
avec des frites	Vous demandez
ah-vek deh freet	*Voo deh-mon-deh*
sur le pain grillé	Ils demandent
s'your le pahn gree-eh	*Eel deh-mond*
pour le petit-déjeuner	Elles demandent
por ler p'tee deh-jher-neh	*El deh-mond*
pour le dîner	pour le dessert
por ler dee-neh	*por ler deh-sairh*

Funny Sentences Using 'Demander'

I ask for a tiger on toast for breakfast.

We ask for a rainbow with chips for dinner.

You (singular) ask for a dinosaur and ketchup for dessert.

Now, can you write your own?
Don't forget to make them funny!

Donner *(don-eh)* To give

Type of verb:
Regular -er

Anglais	Français	Say it!
I give	**Je donne**	*Jher don*
You give (informal singular)	**Tu donnes**	*Too don*
He gives	**Il donne**	*Eel don*
She gives	**Elle donne**	*El don*
We give	**Nous donnons**	*Noo don-ohn*
You give (formal singular and ALL plurals)	**Vous donnez**	*Voo don-eh*
They give (plural, if any are males)	**Ils donnent**	*Eel don*
They give (plural, if all are female)	**Elles donnent**	*El don*

Extra Vocabulary		
a bouquet	**un bouquet**	*uhn boo-keh*
a box	**une boîte**	*oon bwaht*
a herd	**un troupeau**	*uhn troo-poh*
of bananas	**de bananes**	*der bah-nanh*
of ducks	**de canards**	*der cah-narh*
of sausages	**de saucisses**	*der soh-seess*
of worms	**de vers**	*der vairh*
(to) the actress	**à l'actrice**	*ah lac-treess*
(to) the headteacher (male)	**au directeur**	*oh dee-rec-terh*
(to) the singer (male)	**au chanteur**	*oh shon-erh*

I give	a bouquet
You give (Informal singular)	a box
He gives	a herd
She gives	of bananas
We give	of ducks
You give (Formal singular and ALL plurals)	of sausages
They give (Plural, where at least one is male)	of worms
They give (Plural, where all are female)	to the actress
to the singer	to the headteacher

un bouquet	**Je donne**
uhn boo-keh	*Jher don*
une boîte	**Tu donnes**
oon bwaht	*Too don*
un troupeau	**Il donne**
uhn troo-poh	*Eel don*
de bananes	**Elle donne**
der bah-nahn	*El don*
de canards	**Nous donnons**
der cah-narh	*Noo don-ohn*
de saucisses	**Vous donnez**
der soh-seess	*Voo don-eh*
de vers	**Ils donnent**
der vairh	*Eel don*
à l'actrice	**Elles donnent**
ah lac-treess	*El don*
au directeur	**au chanteur**
oh dee-rec-terh	*oh shon-terh*

Funny Sentences Using 'Donner'

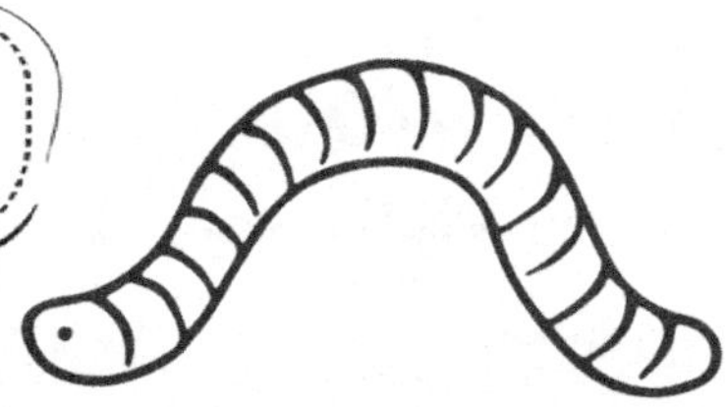

I give a bouquet of sausages to the headteacher.

He gives the actress a herd of bananas.

You (singular) give a box of worms to the singer.

Now, can you write your own?
Don't forget to make them funny!

Jouer *(jhoo-eh)* To play

Type of verb:
Regular -er

Anglais	Français	Say it!
I play	**Je joue**	*Jher jhoo*
You play (informal singular)	**Tu joues**	*Too jhoo*
He plays	**Il joue**	*Eel jhoo*
She plays	**Elle joue**	*El jhoo*
We play	**Nous jouons**	*Noo jhoo-ohn*
You play (formal singular and ALL plurals)	**Vous jouez**	*Voo jhoo-eh*
They play (plural, if any are males)	**Ils jouent**	*Eel jhoo*
They play (plural, if all are female)	**Elles jouent**	*El jhoo*

Extra Vocabulary		
basketball	**au basket-ball**	*oh bask-et-bool*
football	**au football**	*oh foot-bool*
golf	**au golf**	*oh golf*
tennis	**au tennis**	*oh teh-neess*
on	**sur**	*s'yourh*
an iceberg	**un iceberg**	*uhn eess-bairhg*
a pirate ship	**un bateau pirate**	*uhn bah-toh pee-hraht*
the Eiffel Tower	**la tour Eiffel**	*lah toorh ee-fel*
Venus	**Vénus**	*veh-nooss*
with ____________	**avec** (Insert the name of a friend/famous person of your choice!)	

I play	basketball
You play (Informal singular)	football
He plays	golf
She plays	tennis
We play	on
You play (Formal singular and ALL plurals)	an iceberg
They play (Plural, where at least one is male)	a pirate ship
They play (Plural, where all are female)	the Eiffel Tower
Venus	with ______ (insert name)

au basketball	**Je joue**
oh bas-ket-bool	*Jher jhoo*
au football	**Tu joues**
oh foot-bool	*Too jhoo*
au golf	**Il joue**
oh golf	*Eel jhoo*
au tennis	**Elle joue**
oh teh-neess	*El jhoo*
sur	**Nous jouons**
s'yourh	*Noo jhoo-ohn*
un iceberg	**Vous jouez**
uhn eess-bairhg	*Voo jhoo-eh*
un bateau pirate	**Ils jouent**
uhn bah-toh pee-hraht	*Eel jhoo*
la tour Eiffel	**Elles jouent**
lah toorh ee-fel	*El jhoo*
avec ___________	**Vénus**
ah-vek	*veh-nooss*

Funny Sentences Using 'Jouer'

I play tennis on an iceberg with ___________. (insert a name)

She plays basketball on a pirate ship with ___________.

They (all boys) play golf on Venus with ___________.

Can you think of funny people to include in your sentences?

Parler (parhl-eh) To talk/speak

Type of verb:
Regular -er

Anglais	Français	Say it!
I talk/speak	Je parle	*Jher parhl*
You talk/speak (informal singular)	Tu parles	*Too parhl*
He likes/talks	Il parle	*Eel parhl*
She likes/talks	Elle parle	*El parhl*
We talk/speak	Nous parlons	*Noo parhl-ohn*
You talk/speak (formal singular and ALL plurals)	Vous parlez	*Voo parhl-eh*
They talk/speak (plural, if any are males)	Ils parlent	*Eel parhl*
They talk/speak (plural, if all are female)	Elles parlent	*El parhl*

Extra Vocabulary		
to the cow	à la vache	*ah lah vash*
to the superhero	au super-héros	*oh soo-pairh-ehr-oh*
to the horse	au cheval	*oh sher-vahl*
to the turtle	à la tortue	*ah lah torh-too*
in the red hat	au chapeau rouge	*oh shah-poh roojh*
in the tutu	en tutu	*ohn too-too*
with wings	avec des ailes	*ah-vek dehz ell-uh (quick uh)*
at the circus	au cirque	*oh seerk*
on the street corner	au coin de la rue	*oh cwahn der lah rhoo*
at the shops	aux magasins	*oh mah-gah-zahn*

I talk

You talk

(Informal singular)

He talks

She talks

We talk

You talk

(Formal singular and ALL plurals)

They talk

(Plural, where at least one is male)

They talk

(Plural, where all are female)

at the shops

to the cow

to the superhero

to the horse

to the turtle

in the red hat

in the tutu

with wings

at the circus

on the street corner

à la vache	**Je parle**
ah lah vash	*Jher parhl*
au super-héros	**Tu parles**
oh soo-pairh-ehr-oh	*Too parhl*
au cheval	**Il parle**
oh sher-val	*Eel parhl*
à la tortue	**Elle parle**
ah lah torh-too	*El parhl*
au chapeau rouge	**Nous parlons**
oh shah-poh roojh	*Noo parhl-ohn*
en tutu	**Vous parlez**
ohn too-too	*Voo parhl-eh*
avec des ailes	**Ils parlent**
ah-vek dehz el	*Eel parhl*
au cirque	**Elles parlent**
oh seerk	*El parhl*
au coin de la rue	**aux magasins**
oh cwahn der lah rhoo	*oh mah-gah-zahn*

Funny Sentences Using 'Parler'

I talk to the cow in the red hat.

We talk to the horse with wings at the circus.

She talks to the superhero in the tutu at the shops.

Now write your own sentences.
How silly can you make them?

Congratulations!

Type of verb: Regular -er

You have now conjugated some regular -er verbs!

This means that you are able to conjugate ANY regular -er verb by following these two easy rules:

1) Simply remove the -er ending from the verb:

parler → **parl**

2) Then add the correct ending, as follows:

Pronoun	Ending	Conjugated Verb
Je	-e	Je parle
Tu	-es	Tu parles
Il	-e	Il parle
Elle	-e	Elle parle
Nous	-ons	Nous parlons
Vous	-ez	Vous parlez
Ils	-ent	Ils parlent
Elles	-ent	Elles parlent

30 –er Verbs

Type of verb:
Regular -er

Here are some -er verbs you can try conjugating yourself!

Verb	Meaning
aider	to help
apporter	to bring
arriver	to arrive
brosser	to brush
chanter	to sing
chercher	to look for
coiffer	to style (hair)
couper	to cut
danser	to dance
dessiner	to draw
écouter	to hear
embrasser	to hug/kiss
fermer	to close
marcher	to walk
nettoyer	to clean

Verb	Meaning
oublier	to forget
passer	to pass
penser	to think
pleurer	to cry
regarder	to watch/look at
rêver	to dream
sauter	to jump
semer	to sow
téléphoner	to call (on phone)
tomber	to fall
travailler	to work
trouver	to find
voler	to fly
visiter	to visit
voyager	to travel

Choisir *(shwah-zeerh)* To choose

Type of verb:
Regular -ir

Anglais	Français	Say it!
I choose	Je choisis	*Jher shwah-zee*
You choose (informal singular)	Tu choisis	*Too shwah-zee*
He chooses	Il choisit	*Eel shwah-zee*
She chooses	Elle choisit	*El shwah-zee*
We choose	Nous choisissons	*Noo shwah-zee-sohn*
You choose (formal singular and ALL plurals)	Vous choisissez	*Voo shwah-zee-seh*
They choose (plural, if any are males)	Ils choisissent	*Eel shwah-zeess*
They choose (plural, if all are female)	Elles choisissent	*El shwah-zeess*

Extra Vocabulary		
to eat	de manger	*der mohn-jheh*
to live (reside)	d'habiter	*dah-bee-teh*
to sleep	de dormir	*der dorh-meerh*
in a cupboard	dans un placard	*dohnz uhn plah-car*
in a pigsty	dans une porcherie	*dohnz oon porh-sherh-ee*
in the shed	dans l'abri de jardin	*dohn lah-bree der jahr-dahn*
in (under) the shower	sous la douche	*soo lah doosh*
every (each) day	chaque jour	*shac jhorh*
on holiday	en vacances	*ohn vah-conss*
at weekends	le week-end	*ler week-end*

I choose	to eat
You choose (Informal singular)	to live
He chooses	to sleep
She chooses	in a cupboard
We choose	in a pigsty
You choose (Formal singular and ALL plurals)	in the shed
They choose (Plural, where at least one is male)	in the shower
They choose (Plural, where all are female)	every day
at weekends	on holiday

de manger

der mohn-jheh

d'habiter

dah-bee-teh

de dormir

der dorh-meerh

dans un placard

dohnz uhn plah-carh

dans une porcherie

dohnz oon porh-sher-ee

dans l'abri de jardin

dohn lah-bree der jahr-dahn

sous la douche

soo lah doosh

chaque jour

shac jhorh

en vacances

ohn vah-conss

Je choisis

Jher shwah-zee

Tu choisis

Too shwah-zee

Il choisit

Eel shwah-zee

Elle choisit

El shwah-zee

Nous choisissons

Noo shwah-zee-sohn

Vous choisissez

Voo shwah-zee-seh

Ils choisissent

Eel shwah-zeess

Elles choisissent

El shwah-zeess

le week-end

ler week-end

Funny Sentences Using 'Choisir'

I choose to sleep in a cupboard at weekends.

She chooses to eat in the shower every day.

They (including a boy) choose to live in a pigsty on vacation.

**Now, can you write your own?
Don't forget to make them funny!**

Finir (fee-neerh) To finish

Type of verb:
Regular -ir

Anglais	Français	Say it!
I finish	**Je finis**	*Jher fee-nee*
You finish (informal singular)	**Tu finis**	*Too fee-nee*
He finishes	**Il finit**	*Eel fee-nee*
She finishes	**Elle finit**	*El fee-nee*
We finish	**Nous finissons**	*Noo fee-nee-sohn*
You finish (formal singular and ALL plurals)	**Vous finissez**	*Voo fee-nee-seh*
They finish (plural, if any are males)	**Ils finissent**	*Eel fee-neess*
They finish (plural, if all are female)	**Elles finissent**	*El fee-neess*

Extra Vocabulary		
the marathon	le marathon	*ler mah-rah-tohn*
burping	de roter	*der rhoh-teh*
juggling	de jongler	*der john-gleh*
galloping	de galoper	*der gah-lop-eh*
yodelling	de jodler	*der jhod-leh*
with the frogs	avec les grenouilles	*ah-vek leh grohn-oo-ee*
with the owls	avec les chouettes	*ah-vek leh shoo-et*
with the pigs	avec les cochons	*ah-vek leh coh-shohn*
at school	à l'école	*ah leh-col*
at the supermarket	au supermarché	*oh soo-pairh-marh-sheh*

I finish	the marathon
You finish (Informal singular)	burping
He finishes	juggling
She finishes	galloping
We finish	yodelling
You finish (Formal singular and ALL plurals)	with the frogs
They finish (Plural, where at least one is male)	with the owls
They finish (Plural, where all are female)	with the pigs
at the supermarket	at school

le marathon	**Je finis**
ler mah-rah-tohn	*Jher fee-nee*
de roter	**Tu finis**
der rhoh-teh	*Too fee-nee*
de jongler	**Il finit**
der john-gleh	*Eel fee-nee*
de galoper	**Elle finit**
der gah-loh-peh	*El fee-nee*
de jodler	**Nous finissons**
der jhod-leh	*Noo fee-nee-sohn*
avec le grenouilles	**Vous finissez**
ah-vek leh grohn-oo-ee	*Voo fee-nee-seh*
avec les chouettes	**Ils finissent**
ah-vek leh shoo-et	*Eel fee-neess*
avec les cochons	**Elles finissent**
ah-vek leh coh-shohn	*El fee-neess*
à l'école	**au supermarché**
ah leh-col	*oh soo-pairh-marh-sheh*

Funny Sentences Using 'Finir'

I finish the marathon with the frogs.

You (plural) finish burping at the supermarket.

We finish yodelling with the pigs at school.

Now, can you write your own?
Don't forget to make them funny!

Congratulations!

Type of verb:
Regular -ir

You have now conjugated some regular -ir verbs!

This means that you are able to conjugate ANY regular -ir verb by following these two easy rules:

1) Simply remove the -ir ending from the verb:

finir → fin

2) Then add the correct ending, as follows:

Pronoun	Ending	Conjugated Verb
Je	-is	Je finis
Tu	-is	Tu finis
Il	-it	Il finit
Elle	-it	Elle finit
Nous	-issons	Nous finissons
Vous	-issez	Vous finissez
Ils	-issent	Ils finissent
Elles	-issent	Elles finissent

30 –ir Verbs

Type of verb:
Regular -ir

Here are some -ir verbs you can try conjugating yourself!

Verb	Meaning
agir	to act
applaudir	to applaud
avertir	to warn
bâtir	to build
embellir	to beautify
établir	to establish
fourir	to furnish/supply
grandir	to grow
grossir	to gain weight
guérir	to heal
haïr	to hate
investir	to invest
jaillir	to gush
jouir	to enjoy
mentir	to lie

Verb	Meaning
nourrir	to feed
obéir	to obey
pâlir	to turn pale
punir	to punish
ralentir	to slow down
remplir	to fill
réfléchir	to think
réunir	to gather
réussir	to succeed
rougir	to blush
salir	to dirty
saluer	to greet
saisir	to grasp
sentir	to feel/smell
vieillir	to grow old

Attendre *(ah-tohn-druh)* To wait

Type of verb:
Regular -re

Anglais	Français	Say it!
I wait	J'attends	*Jh'ah-tohn*
You wait (informal singular)	Tu attends	*Too ah-tohn*
He waits	Il attend	*Eel ah-tohn*
She waits	Elle attend	*El ah-tohn*
We wait	Nous attendons	*Nooz ah-tohn-dohn*
You wait (formal singular and ALL plurals)	Vous attendez	*Vooz ah-tohn-deh*
They wait (plural, if any are males)	Ils attendent	*Eelz ah-tohnd*
They wait (plural, if all are female)	Elles attendent	*Elz ah-tohnd*

Extra Vocabulary		
the chicken	la poule	*lah pool*
the fairy	la fée	*lah feh*
the giant	le géant	*ler jheh-ohn*
the goat	la chèvre	*lah shev-ruh (short uh)*
in high heels	en talons hauts	*ohn tah-lohn oh*
in the onesie	en grenouillère	*ohn grohn-ooee-airh*
in the snorkel	en tuba	*ohn too-bah*
in the sombrero	en sombrero	*ohn som-brair-hoh*
at the castle	au château	*oh shah-toh*
at the football match	au match de football	*oh match der foot-bool*

I wait	the chicken
You wait (Informal singular)	the fairy
He waits	the giant
She waits	the goat
We wait	in high heels
You wait (Formal singular and ALL plurals)	in the onesie
They wait (Plural, where at least one is male)	in the snorkel
They wait (Plural, where all are female)	in the sombrero
at the football match	at the castle

la poule	J'attends
lah pool	*Jhah-tohn*
la fée	**Tu attends**
lah feh	*Too ah-tohn*
le géant	**Il attend**
ler jheh-ohn	*Eel ah-tohn*
la chèvre	**Elle attend**
lah shev-ruh (short uh)	*El ah-tohn*
en talons hauts	**Nous attendons**
ohn tah-lohn oh	*Nooz ah-tohn-dohn*
en grenouillère	**Vous attendez**
ohn grohn-ooee-airh	*Vooz ah-tohn-deh*
en tuba	**Ils attendent**
ohn too-bah	*Eelz ah-tohnd*
en sombrero	**Elles attendent**
ohn som-brair-hoh	*Elz ah-tohnd*
au château	**au match de football**
oh shah-toh	*oh match der foot-bool*

Funny Sentences Using 'Attendre'

I wait for the chicken in high heels.

They (all boys) wait for the giant in the snorkel at the castle.

You (plural) wait for the fairy in the sombrero at the football match.

Now, can you write your own? Don't forget to make them funny!

Répondre *(reh-pond-ruh)* To answer

Type of verb:
Regular -re

Anglais	Français	Say it!
I reply	Je réponds	*Jher reh-pohn*
You reply (informal singular)	Tu réponds	*Too reh-pohn*
He replies	Il répond	*Eel reh-pohn*
She replies	Elle répond	*El reh-pohn*
We reply	Nous répondons	*Noo reh-pohn-dohn*
You reply (formal singular and ALL plurals)	Vous répondez	*Voo reh-pohn-deh*
They reply (plural, if any are males)	Ils répondent	*Eel reh-pohnd*
They reply (plural, if all are female)	Elles répondent	*Elz reh-pohnd*

Extra Vocabulary		
to the doctor	au médecin	*oh mehd-sahn*
to the gerbil	à la gerbille	*ah lah jhair-beel*
to the king	au roi	*oh rh-wah*
to the witch	à la sorcière	*ah lah sor-see-airh*
by mooing	en meuglant	*ohn merg-lohn*
by neighing	en hennissant	*ohn en-ee-sohn*
by quacking	en cancanant	*ohn cohn-can-ohn*
by whispering	en chuchotant	*ohn shoo-shoh-tohn*
loudly	fortement	*fort-mohn*
quietly	doucement	*dooss-mohn*

I reply	to the doctor
You reply (Informal singular)	to the gerbil
He replies	to the king
She replies	to the witch
We reply	by mooing
You reply (Formal singular and ALL plurals)	by neighing
They reply (Plural, where at least one is male)	by quacking
They reply (Plural, where all are female)	by whispering
quietly	loudly

au médecin	**Je réponds**
oh mehd-sahn	*Jher reh-pohn*
à la gerbille	**Tu réponds**
ah lah jhair-beel	*Too reh-pohn*
au roi	**Il répond**
oh rh-wah	*Eel reh-pohn*
à la sorcière	**Elle répond**
ah lah sor-see-airh	*El reh-pohn*
en meuglant	**Nous répondons**
ohn merg-lohn	*Noo reh-pohn-dohn*
en hennissant	**Vous répondez**
ohn en-ee-sohn	*Voo reh-pohn-deh*
en cancanant	**Ils répondent**
ohn cohn-can-ohn	*Eel reh-pohnd*
en chuchotant	**Elles répondent**
ohn shoo-shoh-tohn	*El reh-pohnd*
fortement	**doucement**
fort-mohn	*dooss-mohn*

Funny Sentences Using 'Répondre'

I reply to the witch by quacking.

You (informal singular) reply to the doctor by mooing loudly.

They (all girls) reply to the king by neighing quietly.

Now, can you write your own?
Don't forget to make them funny!

Congratulations!

Type of verb: Regular -re

You have now conjugated some regular -re verbs!

This means that you are able to conjugate ANY regular -re verb by following these two easy rules:

1) Simply remove the -re ending from the verb:

répondre → repond

2) Then add the correct ending, as follows:

Pronoun	Ending	Conjugated Verb
Je	-s	Je réponds
Tu	-s	Tu réponds
Il	-	Il répond
Elle	-	Elle répond
Nous	-ons	Nous répondons
Vous	-ez	Vous répondez
Ils	-ent	Ils répondent
Elles	-ent	Elles répondent

More –re Verbs

Type of verb:
Regular -re

-re verbs are a smaller class of verbs, so there are not so many. However, here is a list of -re verbs you can learn to conjugating yourself!

Verb	Meaning
confondre	to confuse
correspondre	to correspond
défendre	to defend
dépendre	to depend
descendre	to descend
entendre	to hear/understand
étendre	to stretch
fondre	to melt
mordre	to bite

Verb	Meaning
pendre	to hang/suspend
perdre	to lose
prétendre	to claim
rendre	to give back
répandre	to spread/scatter
suspendre	to suspend
tordre	to twist
vendre	to sell

You're a French Champion!

Congratulations

____

on completing the

Funny French Sentences Workbook for Kids

From the Team at Kingsnorth Kids!

Date: ____________________

Answers

Page 13 - Être

Je suis sur Mars pour skier avec des singes.

Elle est à la fête pour danser avec des extraterrestres.

Il est à la piscine pour jouer au cache-cache avec les dauphins.

Page 17 - Avoir

J'ai des éléphants sous le lit.

Elles ont des chaussettes qui dansent le ballet sur le toit.

Vous avez des hippopotames qui se cachent dans l'armoire.

Page 21 - Faire

Je fais du bruit avec un robot.

Ils font les courses avec un astronaute.

Tu fais un voyage avec un crocodile.

Page 25 - Aller

Je vais à la Lune.

Tu vas en vacances à la bibliothèque.

Il va à l'école à dos de licorne.

Page 29 - Dire

Il dit des blagues au vampire.

Elle dit bonjour au narval aux cheveux verts.

Vous dites salut au clown aux yeux roses.

Page 33 - Vouloir

Je veux sautiller avec des pirates.

Ils veulent patiner avec des sirènes.

Nous voulons chanter avec des gorilles.

Page 37 - Pouvoir

Il peut voler comme un serpent.

Tu peux nager comme un panillon dans la mer.

Elle peut courir comme une baleine dans le ciel.

Page 41 - Manger

Je mange du fromage et de la glace.

Elle mange des bananes avec du poisson.

Vous mangez du gateau et des pommes de terre avec de la boue.

Page 45 - Boire

Je bois du lait dans un arrosoir.

Tu bois du café dans un bocal à poissons.

Elles boivent du thé dans une poêle.

Page 49 - Voir

Je vois un paresseux jouer du piano.

Il voit un lion faire du yoga au clair de lune.

Ils voient une méduse faire des claquettes dans le bain.

53 - Devoir

Je dois porter une armure et des palmes.

Ils doivent porter une robe de bal et des pantoufles à la fête.

Nous devons porter un kit de football, des pantoufles et une couronne chez le dentiste.

Page 57 - Aimer

J'aime l'odeur des cochons quand il neige.

Elles aiment la sensation des escargots quand il fait beau.

Vous aimez le gout des araignées quand il pleut.

Answers

Page 61 - Demander

Je demande un tigre sur du pain-grillé pour le petit-déjeuner.

Nous demandons un arc-en-ciel avec des frites pour le dîner.

Tu demandes un dinosaure et du ketchup pour le dessert.

Page 65 - Donner

Je donne un bouquet de saucisses au directeur.

I donne à l'actrice un troupeau de bananes.

Tu donnes une boîte de vers au chanteur.

Page 69 - Jouer

Je joue au tennis sur un iceberg avec __________.

Elle joue au basket-ball sur un bateau pirate avec __________.

Ils jouent au golf sur Vénus avec __________.

Page 73 - Parler

Je parle à la vache au chapeau rouge.

Nous parlons au cheval avec des ailes au cirque.

Elle parle au superhéros en tutu aux magasins.

Page 79 - Choisir

Je choisis de dormir dans un placard le weekend.

Elle choisit de manger sous la douche chaque jour.

Ils choisit d'habiter dans une porcherie en vacances.

Page 83 - Finir

Je finis le marathon avec les grenouilles.

Vous finissez de roter au supermarché.

Nous finissons de jodler avec les cochons à l'école.

Page 89 - Attendre

J'attends la poule en talons hauts.

Ils attendent le géant en tuba au chateau.

Vous attendez la fée en sombrero au match de football.

Page 93 - Répondre

Je réponds à la sorcière en cancanant.

Tu rèponds au médecin en meuglant forcement.

Elles répondent au roi en hennissant doucement.

French Phonics - Vowels

French has many different sounds. Don't worry , this is just for reference.
All pronunciations will be given!

Here are the basic French vowel (a, e, i, o, u) sounds.

a à â	a short **ah** sound. The **â** sound is slightly longer than the others.	le chat là la hâte	the cat there haste
ai aî ei	An **e** sound, as in **egg**.	la laine fraîche seize	the wool fresh sixteen
au eau	An **oh** sound, as in **rose**.	jaune l'eau	yellow the water
e è	An **e** sound, as in the middle of **hair**.	la mer le frère	the sea the brother
ê	An **e** sound, as in **egg**.	la grève	the strike
e	At the end of a short word, **er**, as in **her**.	le	the (masc.)
e	Silent at the end of other words.	la table	the table
eu oeu	An **er** sound, as in **her**.	bleu l'oeuf	blue the egg
i î y	A short **ee** sound, as in **feet**.	le midi l'abîme il y a	midday the abyss there is/are
o	a short **o**, as in **hot**.	la poste	Post Office
ô	An **oh** sound, as in **rose**.	l'hôtel	the hotel
oi	A **wah** sound.	le poids	the weight
ou u	An **oo** sound. There is no actual English sound for **ou**, but **oo** is close enough!	au bout de j'ai vu	at the end of I saw

French Phonics - Consonants

Some consonants (all other letters except a, e, i, o and u) also make different sounds than in English. Here are the sounds that are different.			
c	A c sound, as in **cat**.	couvrir	to cover
c	**s**, if followed by **e**, **i**, **or**, **y**, as in English.	cinq	five
ç	An **s** sound, as in **soup**.	ça	that
ch	A **sh** sound, as in **shoe**.	le chat	the cat
g	A **g** sound, as in **go**.	gris	grey
g	A soft **jh** sound, like the **s** in **treasure**, after **e**, **i** or **y**	le gym	the gym
h	This sound is **ALWAYS silent**.	l'hôtel	the hotel
j	A soft **jh** sound, like the **s** in **treasure**.	je	I
qu	A k sound, as in **king**.	qui	who
r	A rasp from the back of the throat, as if clearing it.	rouge	red
s	Usually an **s** sound, as in **soup**.	la soupe	soup
s	Between two vowels, it becomes a **z** sound, as in **zebra**.	plaisir	pleasure

Although the last letters of French words are not usually pronounced, sometimes they are, usually when followed by a vowel. These are called **liaisons**, and you may notice some of these in the pronunciations in this book!

French Phonics - Nasal Sounds

Some letters make a different sound in French because they are said from the nose. Don't worry too much about this - you will still be understood if you can't say these sounds properly.
Try to imagine you have a blocked nose when saying these!

om	An **om** sound, as in **Tom**, with the **m** hardly pronounced.	le nom	the name
on	An **ong** sound, as in **long**, with the **ng** hardly pronounced.	mon	my (masc.)
un	An **ung** sound, as in **hung**, with the **ng** hardly pronounced.	un	a (masc.)
am em	An **om** sound, as in **Tom**, with the **m** hardly pronounced.	le jambon decembre	the ham December
an en	An **ong** sound, as in **long**, with the **ng** hardly pronounced.	l'an entrer	the year to enter
aim	An **am** sound, as in **Sam**, with the **m** hardly pronounced.	avoir faim	to be hungry
im	An **am** sound, as in **Sam**, with the **m** hardly pronounced.	le timbre	the stamp
in ain ein	An **an** sound, as in **tan**, with the **n** hardly pronounced.	le pin du pain plein	the pine some bread full (masc.)
ien	An **ee-ang** sound, with the **ng** hardly pronounced.	rien	nothing

A-Z Vocabulary List

adventure	une aventure
alien	un extraterrestre
astronaut	un astronaute
at	à
ball gown	la robe de bal
ballet	le ballet
banana	la banane
bananas	les bananes
basket	le panier
bath	le bain
beach	la plage
bed	le lit
breakfast	le petit-déjeuner
bucket	le seau
burp	roter
box	la boîte
bouquet	le bouquet
butterfly	le papillon
camel	le chameau
cake	le gâteau
castle	le château
cheese	le fromage
chicken	le poulet
circus	le cirque
clown	le clown
coffee	le café
cow	la vache
crocodile	le crocodile
crown	la couronne

cupboard	le placard
day	le jour
dentist	le dentiste
dinner	le dîner
dinosaur	le dinosaure
doctor	le docteur
dolphin	le dauphin
ducks	les canards
each	chaque
Eiffel Tower	la tour Eiffel
egg	l'œuf
elephant	l'éléphant
eyes	les yeux
fairy	la fée
farm	la ferme
film star	la vedette
fish	le poisson
fish bowl	le bocal à poissons
flippers	les palmes
football	le football
football kit	le kit de football
football match	le match de football
fries	les frites
frog	la grenouille
frying pan	la poêle
gallop	galoper
gerbil	la gerbille
giant	le géant
giraffe	la girafe

give	donner
go	aller
goat	la chèvre
golf	le golf
gorilla	le gorille
green	vert(e)
hair	les cheveux
hat	le chapeau
have	avoir
have to	devoir
headteacher (male)	le directeur
hello	bonjour
herd	le troupeau
hi	salut
hippo	l'hippopotame
high heels	les talons hauts
hide-and-seek	le cache-cache
horse	le cheval
hot chocolate	le chocolat chaud
ice cream	la glace
iceberg	l'iceberg
in	dans
it is sunny	il fait soleil
it rains/it is raining	il pleut
it snows/it is snow-ing	il neige
jellyfish	la méduse
joke	la blague
jump	sauter
juggle	jongler
ketchup	le ketchup
king	le roi

knit	tricoter
library	la bibliothèque
like/love	aimer
lion	le lion
live (reside)	habiter
loudly	fortement
make /do	faire
marathon	le marathon
Mars	Mars
mermaid	la sirène
milk	le lait
monkey	le singe
moo	meugler
moon	la lune
moonlight	le clair de lune
mountain	la montagnes
mud	la boue
narwhal	le narval
neigh	hennir
noise	le bruit
nose	le nez
on	sur
onesie	la grenouillère
orange juice	le jus d'orange
owl	la chouette
parrot	le perroquet
party	la fête
piano	le piano
pig	le cochon
pigsty	la porcherie
pink	rose

pirate	le pirate
pirate ship	le bateau pirate
play	jouer
potato	la pomme de terre
quietly	doucement
rain	la pluie
rainbow	l'arc-en-ciel
red	rouge
reply	répondre
robot	le robot
roof	le toit
run	courir
sausage	la saucisse
say	dire
school	l'école
sea	la mer
see	voir
shed	la cabane
shop	le magasin
shower	la douche
sing	chanter
skate	patiner
skip (along)	sautiller
ski	skier
sky	le ciel
sleep	dormir
slippers	parler
sloth	le paresseux
snake	le serpent
snail	l'escargot (masc.)
snorkel	le tuba
sock	la chaussette

soldier	le soldat
sombrero	le sombrero
spider	l'araignée
street corner	le coin de rue
suit of armor	l'armure
superhero	le superhéros
swimming pool	la piscine
talk/speak	parler
tap dance	faire des claquettes
tea	le thé
tennis	le tennis
the cooking	la cuisine
the feel	la sensation
the shopping	les courses
the singer (male)	le chanteur
the smell	l'odeur
the taste	le goût
the washing up	la vaisselle
tiger	le tigre
toast	le pain grillé
to ask	demander
to be	être
to be able to	pouvoir
to burp	roter
to choose	choisir
to dance	danser
to do	faire
to drink	boire
to eat	manger
to finish	finir
to fly	voler
to gallop	galoper

to give	donner
to go	aller
to have	avoir
to have to	devoir
to hide	cacher
to juggle	jongler
to jump	sauter
to knit	tricoter
to like/love	aimer
to live (reside)	habiter
to make	faire
to moo	meugler
to neigh	hennir
to play	jouer
to quack	cancaner
to reply	répondre
to run	courir
to say	dire
to see	voir
to sing	chanter
to skate	patiner
to skip (along)	sautiller
to ski	skier
to sleep	dormir
to talk/speak	parler
to tap dance	faire des claquettes
to wait	attendre
to want	vouloir
to wear	porter
to whisper	chuchoter
to yodel	yodeler
trip/journey	voyage

trumpet	la trompette
turtle	la tortue
tutu	le tutu
unicorn	la licorne
under	dessous
vampire	le vampire
Venus	Vénus
wardrobe	la garde-robe
watering can	l'arrosoir
weekend	le week-end
whale	la baleine
when	quand
whisper	chuchoter
wings	les ailes
with	avec
witch	la sorcière
worm	le ver
yodel	yodeler
yoga	le yoga
zebra	zèbre le zèbre

Find all our books quickly and easily on your local retailers, no matter where you are in the world, using our Linktree page!

Simply scan the QR code with your phone camera and click the link that appears on the screen beneath the scan. All our books will appear and, if you click on them, it will automatically show links to where you can buy them locally to you!

The Beginner's
Book One
FRENCH
You're a Spanish Star!
has completed all the units in
The Complete Beginner's Spanish Workbook for Kids
Many congratulations!
From the team at Kingsnorth Kids!
Date:
Ages 7+
Workbook for Kids
KINGSNORTH KIDS

About the Author

Jo Chant qualified as a teacher in 1993. She has worked as Head of Modern Foreign Languages at her school for over 15 years, including helping in the training of new leaders in other schools.

As well as being a qualified teacher, she has a Languages degree and a qualification in Special Educational Needs. She has studied and worked overseas in various countries, and has worked at universities, both at home and overseas.

Jo has written a range of novels under various pen names, as well as other Language books.

She still works full time as a teacher, and loves writing books in her spare time. She is a complete bookworm and has a massive library, which nobody appreciates except her!

Printed in Dunstable, United Kingdom

66425419R00065